no reason to hide

/workbook/

Erwin W. Lutzer

HARVEST HOUSE PUBLISHERS
EUGENE, OREGON

All Scripture quotations are taken from The ESV® Bible (The Holy Bible, English Standard Version®), copyright © 2001 by Crossway, a publishing ministry of Good News Publishers. Used by permission. All rights reserved.

Italics in Scripture quotations indicate author's emphasis.

Cover design by Studio Gearbox, David Carlson

Cover photo © WR7 / Shutterstock

Interior design by KUHN Design Group

For bulk, special sales, or ministry purchases, please call 1-800-547-8979. Email: Customerservice@hhpbooks.com

This logo is a federally registered trademark of the Hawkins Children's LLC. Harvest House Publishers, Inc., is the exclusive licensee of this trademark.

No Reason to Hide Workbook
Copyright © 2022 by Erwin W. Lutzer
Published by Harvest House Publishers
Eugene, Oregon 97408
www.harvesthousepublishers.com

ISBN 978-0-7369-8689-2 (pbk)
ISBN 978-0-7369-8690-8 (eBook)

Printed in the United States of America

22 23 24 25 26 27 28 29 30 / VP / 10 9 8 7 6 5 4 3 2 1

Contents

Surrender, Sink, or Swim

Christians are finding it more challenging than ever to interact with others in today's culture. In a world that says there is no objective truth, but rather, each individual has their own "truth" based on their life experiences, Christians are told they're intolerant for claiming that God and His Word are the sole sources of truth for all humanity.

The difficulty is this: In a society that refuses to acknowledge the existence of objective truth, there are no longer any reference points for determining right from wrong, or truth from error. Therefore, for a Christian to speak up about matters such as sin and wrongdoing is considered intolerant. After all, every person is entitled to their own viewpoint, which should never be questioned.

So widespread is this cultural thinking that there is tremendous pressure on Christians to keep their perspectives to themselves. At one time, being considerate of others still allowed room for people to share their differing views with one another without animosity. But that isn't the case anymore.

This puts Christians in a difficult place. For the sake of keeping the peace, the temptation is great for us to simply keep quiet and stay hidden. We may reason, *Wouldn't it be better to not upset people lest they end up with a negative view of Christianity?*

But is that the calling we've been given? Even as culture makes it more costly for us to speak up for the truth, we must ask ourselves: Are we living to please people or to please God?

THE NEED FOR HEROES

Surrender, sink, or swim to the shore.
Sometimes heroes are made because of their courage;
sometimes they are made by their circumstances. Sometimes
a person volunteers to become a hero; sometimes a person
becomes a hero because necessity demands it.

No Reason to Hide, page 16

What did John F. Kennedy do that made him so heroic?

Describe a memorable situation in which you had to make a choice between surrendering, sinking, or swimming.

What would surrender have looked like?

What would sinking have looked like?

What would swimming have looked like?

Regardless of how you responded, what was the most important lesson you learned from that experience?

Read Acts 4:13–21. What did the religious leaders in Jerusalem command Peter and John to do (verse 18)?

How did Peter and John respond (verses 19–20)?

According to verse 21, what was the result of Peter and John's boldness?

In what way does Peter and John's example inspire you?

God has lessons to teach us even as we find ourselves drifting in open waters we have never navigated before.

No Reason to Hide, page 17

Think about a way that God confirmed His faithfulness to you when you felt as if you were adrift. What did God do to help you?

CHRISTIANS AND POLITICS

In *No Reason to Hide*, we read, "Politics cannot be separated from morality, and morality cannot be separated from Christianity" (page 18). Try to give one or two examples of why this statement is true.

I understand the tension we as Christians feel. We would prefer not to become involved in politics or culture wars. We want to be known as loving and caring, and we want to be known for what we support, not for what we are against. We want to be known as being apolitical for a reason; we don't want to allow what appears to be secondary disagreements to divide us. We don't want to erect needless stumbling blocks for the gospel. I agree that sometimes neutrality is best; but at other times it's not possible. Sometimes political issues force us into a moral corner where we must choose sides.

No Reason to Hide, page 20

Jonathan Edwards is cited as believing that "Christians should join forces with non-Christians in the public square to work toward common moral goals" (see page 18 in *No Reason to Hide*). What are at least two examples of moral goals we can work toward with unbelievers—moral goals that are consistent with Scripture?

What are the possible benefits of working on common moral goals with non-Christians in the political or social realms?

What are some ways we as believers can offer hope and grace to a weary and angry world?

Do you think it is possible for Christianity to survive and be a positive influence in an oppressive, anti-Christian political environment? Why or why not?

Matthew 5:11 says, "Blessed are you when others revile you and persecute you and utter all kinds of evil against you falsely *on my account*." Note that if we're attacked for righteousness's sake or for Christ's sake, that counts as persecution. But if we face opposition *apart* from our faith, that doesn't count as persecution. Why is this an important distinction for us to recognize?

In 1 Peter 4:16, we read, "If anyone suffers as a Christian, let him not be ashamed, but let him glorify God in this matter." This is a good passage to remember at the times you are fearful about being embarrassed in front of others because of your faith.

Why should we not be ashamed when others deride or mock us as believers?

How does Peter say we should response instead?

> Our collapsing culture must always be seen through the lens
> of our gospel witness…the opposition we experience often
> positions us for new opportunities to witness about our faith.
>
> *No Reason to Hide*, page 21

Can you give an example of an area in your life where you are facing opposition that could be turned into an opportunity to share your faith? What specific steps can you take?

THE CHURCH IS FACING A DAY OF RECKONING

Let us take time to ponder and answer the questions on page 22 in *No Reason to Hide*. For the sake of personal application, the questions are modified here:

What can we do to prepare ourselves for the days ahead, rather than simply do church as usual?

What can you do to ensure that when unbelievers look at you, they see genuine humility rather than self-righteousness?

Why are love, courage, and humility all so very important as you represent Christ to a watching world?

What can we do to leave a helpful legacy for the believers who follow after us?

Increasingly, Christians are finding it difficult to stay in that "mushy middle."
The fearful are going in one direction, the faithful are going in another.

No Reason to Hide, page 22

What will it take for us to avoid staying in the "mushy middle," and instead, be one who swims?

BEHIND CLOSED DOORS

After the crucifixion, the disciples hid, in fear, behind locked doors. But then Jesus came into their midst, and that changed everything. Their fear melted away, and they became bold witnesses for the Lord.

What Scripture passages contain promises or truths that help to fill you with courage? Try to come up with at least three:

—

—

—

WHY THIS BOOK?

On pages 25-26 of *No Reason to Hide*, we read that "evil never retreats on its own; it only retreats when a greater force is applied against it." What does this mean for how our cultural battles should be fought?

What spiritual resources do we have to counter evil?

This book…is a call for all of us to be *in* the world but
not *of* the world, to confront the culture yet not be contaminated by it.
It is a call to remind us that it's not about us, but about Christ.
And a reminder that we are His representatives.
Like the early church, we must be attractive to the world and expect to
also be hated by it. Unbelievers should be attracted to us as a loving
community but repelled by our biblical standards of holy living.

No Reason to Hide, page 27

Romans 8:31 wonderfully reminds us, "If God is for us, who can be against us?" Yes, we can expect life in today's world to be filled with struggles and challenges. What good can we gain from being believers who, rather than surrender or sink, are committed to swimming?

A Hero Who Found No Reason to Hide

The apostle Peter went from denying Christ three times to being a courageous witness. He wrote, "Rejoice insofar as you share Christ's sufferings, that you may also rejoice and be glad when his glory is revealed. If you are insulted for the name of Christ, you are blessed, because the Spirit of glory and of God rests upon you" (1 Peter 4:13–14).

In what ways are you encouraged by what Peter wrote?

What fears can you lift up to God right now, and ask Him to replace with courage?

Will We Be Intimidated by Collective Demonization?

Peer pressure has always been powerful.

These days, it is even more so. In schools and workplaces, certain ways of thinking are praised, while other ways are soundly condemned. Both traditional media and social media define what views are considered acceptable and what aren't.

If you go with the flow of secular culture, you'll be welcomed with open arms. But if you go against the tide, there will be a price to pay.

In a world driven by large social media platforms, a refusal to go with the crowd can get a lot of negative attention. With a few clicks, suddenly you can find yourself at the center of a firestorm of condemnation for saying or doing something that doesn't meet with culture's approval.

There are times when the potential backlash could be so widespread or intense that we choose to censor ourselves. In fear, we hide our true convictions, knowing that to express them will stir the wrath of others. That's how collective demonization works: Those who are politically correct or woke will band together to vilify and shame the few who dare to express a contrary opinion.

Everyone is expected to applaud what is culturally acceptable. And woe to anyone who refuses to clap.

BEHIND THE BERLIN WALL

"Woke-washing" is a term used to describe companies or stores
that take a radical leftist position on racial or political issues as a
pretense that they are "all in," standing in solidarity with the leftists'
agenda to remake society. They want to be seen as advocates, as
those who are innocent of all the evils attributed to others.

No Reason to Hide, page 36

Based on what you have observed, give one or two examples of popular leftist positions that have gotten the backing of major businesses or organizations.

What is your reaction when a Christian is bold enough to go against the cultural tide?

Today's moral revolution says, "If we can't control you, we will destroy you." Why do you think secular leftists resort so frequently to pressure tactics like collective demonization?

In woke culture, ideology is viewed as being more important than competency. What are the potential negative consequences of this kind of thinking?

THE MARRIAGE OF BIG TECH
AND BIG GOVERNMENT

What is the resulting danger when big tech sees its role as advocating leftist government agendas?

Big tech's rule is simple: Amplify the voices you agree with, and silence those with whom you disagree. What are some examples of voices that you've seen being advocated?

What are some examples of voices that you've seen being silenced?

The runaway slave Frederick Douglass observed that free speech "is the dread of tyrants…it is the one right which they first of all strike down" (see page 43 in *No Reason to Hide*). Why is free speech such a threat to those who want control over others?

What is collective demonization? It is the punishment of all who dare to disagree with those in power; it is the erasure of individualism by stigmatizing and punishing dissenters.

No Reason to Hide, page 44

A WARNING FROM THOSE WHO UNDERSTAND

On page 45 of *No Reason to Hide*, we read these words from Alexei Navalny: "We have seen many examples in Russia and China of such private companies becoming the state's best friends and enablers when it comes to censorship."[1]

Is the fact that major businesses—including big tech companies—are helping to enable government censorship a reason for us to be concerned? Why or why not?

Jesus predicted that families would be *divided* because of Him, and "a person's enemies will be those of his own household" (Matthew 10:36). He also warned His followers they would be "put…to death, and you will be *hated* by all nations for my name's sake. And then many will fall away and *betray* one another and hate one another" (Matthew 24:9–10).

Notice that Jesus talked about what we see happening in our present-day culture: *division, hatred,* and *betrayal.* All three of these dominate much of social media and cultural and political discourse. We are not where some totalitarian countries are, but we appear to be on our way.

No Reason to Hide, pages 44-45

Also on page 45, we read, "If we continue to go in this direction, *that which is cancelled today will be criminalized tomorrow*." Based on what the secular left criticizes and cancels these days, what views and actions do you think have the potential to end up being criminalized in the future?

THE SEARCH FOR EXTREMISTS

In recent years, what has happened to the definitions of the terms *white supremacist* and *extremist*?

Under the radical left's new definition of *extremist*, who are some of the people that have been branded as extremists?

PATRIOTISM'S BLESSINGS

What distinguishes simple patriotism from Christian nationalism?

On page 49 of *No Reason to Hide*, we read, "The divide is not so much between Republican or Democrat, or right versus left; rather, our choices are becoming good versus evil, right versus wrong, freedom versus censorship." In what ways do you see these choices evident in your interactions with culture?

Also on page 49, we're reminded that "in the midst of the chaos, we are to be representatives of Christ. Ultimately, it is the gospel that matters most." Why is being a good representative of Christ the most powerful influence we can have in today's culture?

HISTORY DOES REPEAT ITSELF

History reveals that the Holocaust had its beginnings in stereotypes, prejudice, exclusion, and dehumanization. Small steps became big ones that led to deadly consequences. What are some small steps you see happening in today's society that could lead to bigger ones?

What is the natural result when government overreach occurs?

VALOR IN TRYING TIMES

What are some of the consequences that Christians face today for holding to their convictions?

THE PRIORITY OF THE GOSPEL

The train has left the station. And we are passengers along
with all the others. We can't stop the train by pacing back and
forth, by going from one end of it to the other. But we can share
the truths of the gospel to all of our fellow passengers.

No Reason to Hide, pages 51-52

In *No Reason to Hide*, we read that "all trains are God's trains." What do you think is meant by this?

At the same time that we stand *against* the culture, it is vital that we stand *above* it and stand for Christ. Why do you think it's so crucial to do both at the same time?

James Emery White is quoted as asking, "Is the ultimate goal a Christian nation or a nation of Christians?" Why is the better answer "a nation of Christians"?

What is the only way this can take place?

What is God's solution to evil?

What has God promised *will* happen in the future, according to Revelation 11:15?

A Promise to Carry with Us

The Lord stood by me and strengthened me, so that through me the message might be fully proclaimed and all the Gentiles might hear it. So I was rescued from the lion's mouth. The Lord will rescue me from every evil deed and bring me safely into his heavenly kingdom. To him be the glory forever and ever. Amen (2 Timothy 4:17–18).

In the above passage, what does the apostle Paul thank God for?

In what ways have you seen God strengthen you and keep you safe in the midst of today's culture?

A Hero Who Found No Reason to Hide

Rod Dreher is quoted as saying, "The ordinary man may not be able to overturn the kingdom of lies, but he can at least say that he is not going to be its loyal subject."[2] Why do you think this is an important mentality for us to have—that even though we may not be able to change what the government is doing, we still refuse to clap?

The doctor who shared Christ with Aleksandr Solzhenitsyn was later killed, and Solzhenitsyn went on to become a witness to millions. What does the doctor's example tell us about the importance of being faithful no matter how small our circles of social influence are?

Action Step

What are some specific, tangible ways that Christians can create a community of support to uphold one another when they are attacked?

Will We Expose the Greatest Lie That Is Our Nation's Most Cherished Delusion?

The greatest lie has been around since the Garden of Eden. It's the lie that the serpent spoke to Eve when he tempted her to eat the forbidden fruit: "Your eyes will be opened, and you will be like God" (Genesis 3:5). The serpent was telling Eve she could be whatever she wanted to be—she could even be like God.

This lie has been passed down through the ages in various forms, and ultimately, allows people to exchange places with God. It's a lie that rejects God's design for mankind as well as God's authority and puts self at the center of one's world. The problem with this is that as a result of mankind's fall into sin, the human heart has become "deceitful above all things and desperately sick" (Jeremiah 17:9). It is for this reason that Jesus said, "Out of the heart proceed evil thoughts, murders, adulteries, fornications, thefts, false witness, blasphemies" (Matthew 15:19). In short, the heart is evil.

In its fallen state, the human heart is incapable of righteousness. This explains why so many people are self-deluded when it comes to the cultural issues of our day. Without God as their moral authority, they will do whatever is right in their own eyes. This is the reason for the rampant confusion regarding sexual and gender issues, the attacks against the traditional family, and all kinds of human strife and discord.

After Adam and Eve fell for the lie, they tried to hide from God. Ever since, mankind has continued to run from God, and people have come up with all sorts of lies that have their origin in the lie that was uttered by the serpent: "You can be whatever you want to be."

THE LIE OF KARL MARX—
THE GOD OF POWER

What statement by Karl Marx appears in the rotunda at Humboldt University in Berlin, Germany?

What is the significance of this statement?

Marx's unique contribution was to shift the notion of the deity of man from the individual to the state.

No Reason to Hide, page 61

How did Karl Marx and Friedrich Engels view people, according to their book *The Communist Manifesto*?

It follows that freedom, certainly freedom of religion, had to be abolished, according to Marx, for the simple reason that citizens can have no higher loyalty than to the state. If there is to be worship, it must be the state that is worshipped. If love exists, it has to be love of the state. The state can tolerate no rivals.

No Reason to Hide, page 62

How did Marx believe history could best be explained?

What was Marx's goal?

What were Marx's views on religion and Christianity?

What did Marx's associate, Friedrich Engels, teach about the traditional family structure?

According to Marx, why did people commit crimes?

How did Benito Mussolini define fascism?

According to fascism or statism, what is the only way to achieve equality?

What do those who hold to Marxist thought say about objective truth?

CULTURAL MARXISM:
THE DECONSTRUCTION OF CULTURE

What is meant by the phrase "the long march through the institutions"?

How does cultural Marxism differ from the kind of Marxism that arose in Russia?

What does *deconstruction* refer to, and what is its purpose?

According to Critical Theory, what is alleged about America's foundational writings?

BUILD BACK BETTER

What has happened as a result of Critical Theory being applied to gender, and what is the goal?

SIGMUND FREUD:
THE GOD OF SEXUAL PLEASURE

What did Freud advocate about sexual pleasure?

What accusation is brought against Christianity with regard to self-expression?

According to Freud's thinking, where does authority have to be moved?

What does "autonomous expressive individualism" refer to?

What does Freud's line of thinking say about children's rights and parental authority?

THE SHOTGUN MARRIAGE OF MARX
AND FREUD: THE POLITICIZATION OF SEX

What has resulted from combining Freud's unrestrained drive for sexuality with Marx's quest for political power?

Today's left says, "My ideas cannot be discussed independently from who I am; therefore, if you disagree with me, it is an attack against my personal identity." Describe one or two ways you have seen this kind of reasoning manifest.

When the radical left says, "I am first and foremost a homosexual, a bisexual, a transsexual, and you cannot welcome me into your community unless you affirm my legitimacy and lifestyle," what, in effect, are they saying?

In summary, what does the statement "To find yourself is to look into yourself" mean?

PROGRESSIVISM'S PREVAILING INFLUENCE

What does Christianity affirm, and what does the left say in response?

How does Benjamin Wiker define progressivism?

What does progressivism seek to destroy, and seek to rebuild upon?

THE IMPLICATIONS OF SELF-WORSHIP

What does everything within a person long for?

From Doctrine to Spirituality

What observation did Jerome P. Blaggett make about the way people think today about religion?

On page 73 of *No Reason to Hide*, we read, "Any god that exists must be redefined to agree with our desires." How have you seen this kind of thinking evident in the world around you?

Spreading Malignant Narcissism

What is narcissism, and how is it expressed?

The Contamination of Public Education

What does the radical left believe about the sexual teaching of a child?

On page 75 of *No Reason to Hide*, we read that "Marxism appeals to takers, not givers." Why do you think that is so?

The Destruction of the Family

Self-worship thrives among those who delude themselves into
thinking there is no god who disagrees with their deepest desires.

No Reason to Hide, page 76

When people let their fallen human desires have the last word in their lives, what are some of the potential negative consequences you can see on the family as a whole?

Why do you think it is inevitable that when people become worshippers of self their view of God will become distorted?

DECEIVE, DESTROY, DEMAND

What two paths are before every person?

A Promise to Carry with Us

> Humble yourselves, therefore, under the mighty hand of God so that at the proper time he may exalt you, casting all your anxieties upon him, because he cares for you (1 Peter 5:6–7).

In all of what we discussed in chapter 3—cultural Marxism, Critical Theory, Freud, and progressivism, the self is placed above God. In light of this, why do you think humility is such an important virtue for Christians to pursue?

A Hero Who Found No Reason to Hide

What did Jesus exemplify when He came to Earth, and what are some of the ways He exhibited this?

Take a moment to read Philippians 2:3–8. What stands out to you most about this passage?

> Do nothing from selfish ambition or conceit, but in humility count others more significant than yourselves. Let each of you look not only to his own interests, but also to the interests of others. Have this mind among yourselves, which is yours in Christ Jesus, who, though he was in the form of God, did not count equality with God a thing to be grasped, but emptied himself, by taking the form of a servant, being born in the likeness of men. And being found in human form, he humbled himself by becoming obedient to the point of death, even death on a cross.

Action Step

What are some ways that, even so very subtly, we may end up putting ourselves at the center of our world instead of God? What can we do to make sure our minds and hearts make everything about Him, and not about us?

Will We Encourage Unity or Create Division by Promoting Diversity, Equity, and Inclusion?

When it comes to issues regarding race, there are no easy answers. So much has happened in the past—and continues to happen today—that makes this a delicate topic.

But thankfully, we do have biblical truths and guidelines that can help us. God has not left us without wisdom. The challenge is that so much of what is said today sounds logical, but actually runs contrary to God's Word.

For those of us who are Christians, what's crucial is that we strive to be sensitive and biblically just. The reason I say *biblically* is just that much of what is advocated in social justice does not line up with scriptural teaching. We'll learn more about that as we make our way through this lesson.

When it comes to race, there are things that have happened in the past that were hurtful and wrong. Yet we must also acknowledge that progress *has* been made. As we survey the Diversity, Equity, and Inclusion (DEI) landscape, we come to realize that we have two choices: Either we can continue to dwell upon the sins of the past and punish the people of the present for what happened long ago, or we can seek to be reconciliatory and see everyone—no matter what their race—as having the potential to build toward a better future.

Many of us can agree on the nature of the problems that have plagued us in the past. What people can't seem to agree on are the solutions. One side is heightening division, while the other is encouraging unity. And ultimately, we have to ask ourselves: Is the solution I'm pursuing helping to bring honor and glory to God? If we leave God out of the picture, we can be certain our efforts to solve race problems are doomed to failure.

The Bible confronts racism by emphasizing our similarities, while recognizing our cultural differences. Scripture tells us there is only one race. God has "made from one man every nation of mankind to live on all the face of the earth" (Acts 17:26). Though we may have different ethnicities, ultimately, there is only one human race. Skin color is one way to divide humanity, but in many ways that's an artificial division.

No Reason to Hide, page 85

THE DESTRUCTIVE INFLUENCE OF DIVERSITY, EQUITY, AND INCLUSION

Diversity, Equity, and Inclusion (DEI) Insists That Deference to Certain Groups Is More Important Than Competency or Merit

What does DEI give deference to?

When it comes to real-life situations, what can be the end result when people are chosen *without* any consideration whatsoever for merit or competency?

Author Rod Dreher wrote, "Equity means treating people unequally, regardless of their skills and achievements, to achieve an ideologically correct result."[3] Explain what is meant by the fact that equity forces people to be treated unequally.

Why can we legitimately say that DEI is "code for discrimination"?

When it comes to selecting people to do something, why is competition beneficial?

The 1619 Project Skews History to Exacerbate the Racial Divide

What claim does the 1619 project make about America?

According to Robert Woodson, what "lethal" narrative is pushed by the 1619 project?

What does Woodson say contributes to educational success among African Americans?

On page 91 in *No Reason to Hide*, we read, "Let's ask what we need to do to bring people to a higher level of achievement instead of lowering the bar to incentivize mediocrity." Can you think of a time in your own life when being pushed to a higher level of achievement had a positive effect on you? What did you learn?

DEI Inflames Divisions and Deconstruction

What was the Weather Underground's goal?

What do the modern "heirs" of the Weather Underground attack?

Why does the left declare war against individualism? Because, as Marx knew, individuals are difficult to control; Marxists believe that allowances cannot be made for an individual's personal conscience and freedom. It's better to categorize people as a group and then label them so they will reinforce a collective consciousness, and those who don't comply can be immediately identified. The goal is to forbid people to act independently of the group, and if they do step out of line, they can be labeled as inauthentic and a betrayal of who they should be. They can be punished for independent thought.

No Reason to Hide, page 94

How does this contrast with Martin Luther King Jr.'s approach?

What proposition is the book *White Fragility* dedicated to?

Why does the left declare war on individualism?

What flawed logic does the left apply to the word *equality*?

On page 95 of *No Reason to Hide*, we read, "Only tyranny can attempt to produce equal outcomes—and it must do so by coercion and freedom-denying laws." Why do you think this is the case?

DEI Inflames Hate, Not Forgiveness

Read the prayer that appears on page 97 in *No Reason to Hide*. What kind of responses do you see such a prayer leading people toward?

The Marxist ideology that divides the world into victims and oppressors while ignoring individual differences works against the betterment of race relations.

No Reason to Hide, page 98

Author Tony Evans observes, "Victimology nurtures an unfocused strain of resentment rooted in a defeatist mentality through which all reality is filtered." Why do you think the left's "perpetual casting" of certain people groups as victims is so detrimental?

Do you agree that when victimhood is encouraged, then seeking ways to overcome victimhood ends up being discouraged? Why?

The Standpoint Theory of Knowledge Destroys the Search for Objective Truth

Why is there no "truth out there" in today's woke culture?

What themes do we see constantly in most of the social justice movement literature?

What does the standpoint theory of knowledge say?

The radical left interprets the Constitution not on the basis of its written words, but on what they allege to be sinister motives. What would happen if we were to apply this theory of interpretation to Scripture?

The text, not one's race or privilege, should be the lens through which we interpret God's Word. In woke theology, however, the intention is to interpret the text to promote wokeness...Objectivity, we are told, is unfair to minorities. Only lived experience is to be trusted, especially if it is the experience of the oppressed.

No Reason to Hide, pages 101–102

The New Woke Community Bank Would Destroy Arithmetic

Why does it not make sense to apply social justice to math?

What does the woke community say is the reason for the view that mathematics is objective?

What is the problem with saying there is no objectivity in a discipline like science or math?

DEI Misuses the System

What has happened as a result of applying theories of equity to matters relating to crime?

When it comes to crime, the police, and minorities, what is the more common-sense approach we ought to have?

Why are Marxists proponents of the Defund the Police movement?

How has "justice reform" been redefined?

MANY MINORITIES REJECT DEI

What are minorities who oppose DEI and Critical Race Theory saying about them?

THE CENTRAL FAILURE OF WOKE THEOLOGY

What serious basic error does woke theology make?

Based on Bible verses you know, why does it not make sense to say one group of people is always guilty, and another group is always innocent merely on the basis of skin color?

A Promise to Carry with Us

Worthy are you to take the scroll and to open its seals, for you were slain, and by your blood you ransomed people for God from every tribe and language and people and nation, and you have made them a kingdom and priests to our God, and they shall reign on the earth (Revelation 5:9–10).

On page 110 of *No Reason to Hide*, we read that CRT *"keeps tearing apart what Jesus died to bring together."* Read 1 Corinthians 12:12–26. What statements in this passage refute the kind of thinking promoted by DEI and CRT?

A Hero Who Found No Reason to Hide

On page 112 of *No Reason to Hide*, read what Voddie Baucham wrote about forgiveness. What do you find most encouraging about his words?

Action Step

Among other things, our marching orders are to love one another with brotherly affection, and to outdo one another in showing honor (Romans 12:10). What one or two ways can you make this become reality within the next few days?

Can We Take Steps to Move Beyond Our History of Racism, Stolen Land, and Collective Guilt?

Today's culture wars have led many Christians to become divided over issues relating to race, justice, and more. Believers have taken different viewpoints on controversial issues and, tragically, they've allowed those issues to divide them. This, in turn, has disrupted their unity in Christ.

When we allow our stand on the issues of the day to take priority over ministering alongside one another as members of the body of Christ, we hurt ourselves, the church, and the Lord Himself. When healthy and respectful dialogue degenerate into infighting and division, the church becomes splintered and ineffective.

We must always be mindful that unbelievers are watching us closely. A divided church is not an attractive church. Even when we hold to different perspectives, we are to pursue unity in Christ. Scripture calls us to have the same mind, the same love, and to be humble (Philippians 2:2–3). We're to "love one another with brotherly affection," and to "live in harmony with one another...never be wise in your own sight" (Romans 12:10, 16).

So as we continue our look at how to respond biblically to the issues of today, let us do so with a commitment to prioritizing what we share in common. On some matters, we might find it difficult to see eye to eye, but we should never find it difficult to honor our Lord together, represent Him well, and speak the gospel message clearly. Let us remember that the battle we need to focus on most is that between good and evil, and that our key purpose as a church is to draw people to God and salvation in Christ.

A WHITEWASHED HISTORY

America is not perfect and never will be. The Founding Fathers knew that, which is why they formed a government with checks and balances to keep any one person (or branch of government) from amassing too much power.

No Reason to Hide, page 118

Author Michael P. Farris observes that the ideals written in the Constitution and other founding documents "were bigger than the men who wrote them."[4] Why is this a good mindset for us to have?

What perspective did Martin Luther King Jr. have when he sought racial reconciliation?

No nation has worked as tirelessly to overcome the dark pages of its past as the United States; and no nation has ever risen to the levels of freedom and economic progress as has this country. Amid failure, setbacks, and disappointments, Americans have tried to keep the aspirations and promises of our Founding Fathers alive.

No Reason to Hide, page 119

On page 121 of *No Reason to Hide*, we read, "We aren't where we should be, but no other nation has spent as much time and effort trying to work toward equal opportunity for all."

In what ways does our sinfulness get in the way of making progress on race issues?

When it comes to making progress on racial issues, what can we as Christians offer that the world cannot?

LAND STOLEN FROM THE NATIVE AMERICANS

What is the prevailing narrative in some schools today with regard to white students?

Leftist racial justice advocates want people to live in perpetual guilt over things that took place centuries ago. What common-sense problems do you see with imposing such guilt on people?

What key point did black author Thomas Sowell make in his book *Discrimination and Disparities?*

Racial justice advocates have forgotten the many examples of Christians in the past who took positive steps toward the fair treatment of minorities. What, for example, did Jonathan Edwards do?

What did David Brainerd do?

When it comes to the history of nations of the past and today, what reality must we face?

LEARNING FROM OTHER COUNTRIES

On page 127 of *No Reason to Hide*, we read, "Sadly, nations are formed by wars, often wars of aggression with disputes over boundaries and territories. God will judge all of these actions appropriately; we simply cannot unscramble the past."

With that in mind, what benefits do you see of letting God take care of the past and us keeping our focus on the present and the future?

OWNING OUR PAST, OR THE
MATTER OF COLLECTIVE GUILT

What problems do you see with telling people they must feel guilty and own a past they were not part of?

Would you describe this kind of guilt as demoralizing or constructive? Why?

What observation did former US president Ronald Reagan make about individual guilt versus collective guilt?

What did the prophet Ezekiel clearly state in Ezekiel 18:20?

THE CHALLENGE FOR THE CHURCH

On page 131 of *No Reason to Hide*, we read of Isaac Adams's observation that "we don't have to agree on everything in order to celebrate our unity in Christ." Why is unity in Christ so important, even more so than where we stand on social issues?

What are some of the things we as Christians should be united over?

WHAT TO THE SLAVE IS
THE FOURTH OF JULY?

What point did Frederick Douglass make about America's Founding Fathers?

At the conclusion of his speech "What to a Slave Is the Fourth of July?," what hopeful call did Douglass make?

A Promise to Carry with Us

He himself is our peace, who has made us both one and has broken down in his flesh *the dividing wall of hostility*…that he might create in himself one new man in place of the two, so making peace, and might reconcile us both to God in one body through the cross, thereby *killing the hostility* (Ephesians 2:14–16).

What exhortations are we given in the following passages?

Psalm 34:14—

Romans 12:18 —

Ephesians 4:1–3 —

A Hero Who Found No Reason to Hide

According to 2 Corinthians 5:17–18, what makes it possible for someone to be transformed as radically as John Perkins?

Action Step

Think of someone you know to whom you could be an "ambassador of reconciliation." Start by praying for that person, then think of small steps you can take to develop a stronger acquaintance or friendship with that person. Seek to be a positive and encouraging influence. Doing this even in small ways can be meaningful and significant.

Another option is to become acquainted with an inner-city ministry that is solidly biblical and seeks the kind of racial reconciliation that honors God and encourages unity. Find out ways you can either pray for or support that ministry.

CHAPTER 6

Will We Be Deceived by the Language Used by the Propagandists?

Sometimes the cultural battles can become so wearying that we lose heart. It's tiring to take a stand against false narratives that are intended to sell an agenda. And that's exactly what leftists want—they want us to surrender or sink rather than swim.

What's made today's battles more challenging than ever is the way the radical left has redefined words so that they have the high moral ground and can silence those who disagree with them. The meanings of words have been altered to control not only the dialogue, but the way people think.

That's what propaganda does—it reshapes people's view of reality. It prioritizes ideology over facts and wins people over by appealing to their desires and using deception. By definition, propaganda is biased or misleading information that is used to promote a particular view or cause.

Propaganda seeks to persuade the emotions rather than the mind. If you pay attention, you'll notice that people will often argue for a cause based on what feels right rather than resorting to factual, rational arguments.

THE SAME WORDS, A DIFFERENT DICTIONARY

To call good evil is only half the task. What is the other half?

How is this other half accomplished?

In brief, propaganda is *telling people what they want to hear, then giving them what you want them to have.*

No Reason to Hide, page 144

What is the goal of propaganda?

On page 144 of *No Reason to Hide*, we read that *"if people can be made to believe a lie, they will live as if the lie were the truth."* Can you think of an example or two of this that you've seen in today's culture?

This retreat into the language of "safe-ism" or "freedom from harm" is intended to close the mouths of those who might disagree with the contemporary *zeitgeist*—that is, the spirit of the age. Certain ideas should not be spoken. The radical left touts its commitment to tolerance, yet their tolerance extends only to the echo of their own voices. As someone has said, they are very *in*tolerant of the three *C*s that shaped America: *Christianity*, the *Constitution,* and *capitalism.*

No Reason to Hide, page 150

SIX WAYS LANGUAGE IS
MANIPULATED BY PROPAGANDA

What did George Orwell mean by the term *Newspeak*?

The Use of Evocative Slogans

What is the purpose of a slogan?

Why does the slogan "the fight for social justice" seem so right?

What does the term *social justice* actually mean, as used by propagandists?

Use Language to Create Reality

Give one or two examples of the way secular culture takes that which is dark and calls it light.

What is one example of the way you've noticed the radical left is using language not to *describe* reality, but to *create* it?

When the goal of language is not truth but ideology
and power, the totalitarian state has arrived.

No Reason to Hide, page 148

Use Words to Suppress the Debate

What is the goal of putting parameters around what people can say?

What are some examples of words you've found yourself not using because you fear what other people might think or say?

What are some ways you see the left telling people to "stay in their lane" when it comes to sharing ideas or opinions?

Shame Those Who Disagree with the Accepted Narrative

How does the radical left view those who disagree with them?

Give an example or two of a secular narrative about Christians that is intended to make Christians look bad or hateful.

Ideology Must Always Trump Facts

When it comes to spreading propaganda, what must be done to facts?

What contrast is seen in the way the media handled the Kyle Rittenhouse story versus the Darrell E. Brooks story?

Propaganda does not just control what is being said, but also what is *not* said.

No Reason to Hide, page 155

Use Honorable Terms but Give Them a Less-Than-Honorable Meaning

What two words are being greatly misused today?

Why are the concepts behind these two words so powerful?

What observation does Tim Keller make about naming something a "justice issue"?

Are equality and justice morally neutral? Explain.

What does Judges 21:25 say was true about the ancient Israelites?

How do you see Judges 21:25 applying to culture today?

What are some examples of true justice, or biblical justice?

In what ways are we equal, and in what ways are we not?

HOW DO WE COUNTER PROPAGANDA?

What should we as Christians pray for as we attempt to avoid propaganda traps?

What does Proverbs 2:1–5 tell us about seeking the truth?

Peel Back the Labels

Why is it so important for us to discern possible hidden meanings behind words and slogans?

When Possible, Use More Than One Source for Your Information

What did Gillian Flynn mean when he wrote, "The truth is malleable; you just need to pick the right expert"?

Share an example of how you've seen truth "bent" to accommodate a narrative or a worldview.

Listen to a Trusted Voice

What is one way we can diminish the chances of being deceived by propaganda?

What is God's Word able to do for us, according to the following passages?

Psalm 19:7—

Proverbs 30:5—

2 Timothy 3:16—

In 1 Corinthians 2:1–5, what does the apostle Paul imply about the "wisdom" of men compared to "the power of God"?

A Promise to Carry with Us

After this I heard what seemed to be *the loud voice of a great multitude* in heaven, crying out, "Hallelujah! Salvation and glory and power belong to our God" (Revelation 19:1).

There is coming a day when propaganda and the false wisdom of mankind will no longer deceive people and lead them astray. God will rule, and truth will reign. What are some of the ways life will be different in God's kingdom, as opposed to what life is like in the present fallen world?

A Hero Who Found No Reason to Hide

When the prophet Micaiah spoke the truth and warned King Ahab and King Jehoshaphat to not go into battle, Ahab had Micaiah put in prison. He didn't want to hear the truth. What are some ways you see people denying the truth today, no matter how obvious it is?

In today's culture, what are some examples of the price Christians have to pay to tell the truth?

Action Step

In practical, everyday terms, what does it mean to buy truth and not sell it?

Will We Compromise with the Christian Left?

Perhaps you've heard people say the Bible is outdated, that it is locked into the culture of the day during which it was written. As the centuries have gone by, mankind is said to have become more enlightened not only in the areas of knowledge and the sciences, but also culturally and religiously. There are those who reason that the church needs to broaden its ways of thinking, that it needs to get in sync with the times, so to speak.

The unfortunate result is that there are those in the church who aren't careful to distinguish between cultural norms and biblical morality. Just because a certain form of sexuality has become viewed as acceptable and just because the Bible says we are to be loving doesn't mean we can abandon the moral guidelines God has provided for us in His Word. To say that Scripture has become increasingly irrelevant from a cultural standpoint is to say we have a God who didn't have the foresight to provide us with a guidebook that would endure through the ages. Such thinking suggests we have a less-than-perfect God and less-than-perfect Scripture.

Either God's moral standards apply for all time, or they don't. Either they inform how we are to live in a fallen world, or they are insufficient to do so.

When we lower our view of God's Word, we open the floodgates for ungodly cultural influences to inundate the church. No matter how sincerely we may believe that the "woke theology" that is taught in the name of love and compassion seems right, if it doesn't line up with the clear teaching of Scripture, we end up undermining the foundation on which the church is to stand, and we compromise the gospel.

A WARNING FROM THE PAST

What did Horatius Bonar write some 150 years ago that makes it seem he could have written his words for today?

According to Lucas Miles, what kind of lumber has been used to construct the Trojan horse of Diversity, Equity, and Inclusion (DEI), which is infiltrating the church today?

An example of theology by opinion appears on page 169 of *No Reason to Hide*. What are a couple other examples you can think of, where popular opinion has compelled a church, ministry, or individual Christian to depart from scriptural standards?

> *Will we interpret the Bible through the lens of culture, or will*
> *we interpret culture through the lens of the Bible?*
>
> ***No Reason to Hide***, page 170

HOW AN EVANGELICAL CHURCH GOES WOKE

Read the letter on pages 170–173 of *No Reason to Hide*. In your opinion, what harmful effects was this woke church having on its congregation?

What should the church have emphasized to its people, and what was it emphasizing instead?

What is likely to happen in a church that gets caught up in cultural trends?

THE DECEPTION OF SOCIAL JUSTICE

Based on what you have read in this chapter so far, would you say that today's definition of social justice lines up with the Bible's definition? Why or why not?

According to Samuel Sey, what is the result of Critical Race Theory?

Biblically defined, what is social justice?

On page 175 of *No Reason to Hide*, we read, *"The gospel is not something to achieve, but a gift to be received."* Why is it so vital for us to have this perspective of the gospel?

FROM WHITE SUPREMACY TO CHRISTIAN SUPREMACY

What harm have Christians been accused of causing?

In your opinion, what misunderstandings do you think are causing unbelievers to unjustly criticize believers?

WHEN LOVE WINS!

What happens when the church shifts from what the Bible says to what people think love requires?

In what ways do you see culture's definition of love and God's definition of love at odds with each other today?

What did Jesus say about love in John 14:15?

In what way did the apostle Paul indict humanity in Romans 1:25?

Biblical love—the love of God—which is indeed a chief attribute of God,
is compatible with the judgment that comes from rejecting God's ways.

No Reason to Hide, page 180

IS COMPROMISE POSSIBLE?

What middle ground are professed LGBTQ Christians trying to achieve?

From a biblical standpoint, why does this middle ground not make sense?

On page 181 of *No Reason to Hide*, we read, "A deceptive view of love leads to a deceptive view of repentance." Why do you think this is the case?

CHRISTIANITY REMADE

According to one poll, nearly 70 percent of those who professed to be born-again Christians said they do not believe that Jesus is the only way to God. Using Scripture, how would you respond to those who hold to this view?

What two issues have led some allegedly Christian leaders to deconstruct their faith?

When a church surrenders to the moral revolution, what leftist views has it come to accommodate?

The progressives want to abandon the harder truths of Christianity, and this, in turn, leads to a horrible deception. Certain biblical teachings are at best ignored, and at worst vilified. But there are eternal consequences for rejecting God's Word. Here is a chilling statement that you will not find as part of the progressives' theology: "If anyone's name was not found written in the book of life, he was thrown into the lake of fire" (Revelation 20:15). We must warn those who use the Bible to find what they are looking for and simply ignore the rest.

No Reason to Hide, pages 185–186

On page 186 of *No Reason to Hide*, we read, "People want the blessing of God without the truth of God." Give an example of a way you've seen this happen.

REACHING OUT TO THOSE WHO
ARE DECONSTRUCTING THEIR FAITH

What are some of the things that churches and Christians have done that have led some to reject Christianity?

Do you agree with the statement that "hard truths must be carried in soft hearts"? What does this look like from a practical perspective?

What attitudes should we strive to show when we speak with those who have been hurt by Christianity?

A Promise to Carry with Us

> Take up the whole armor of God, that you may be able to withstand in the evil day, and having done all, to stand firm. Stand therefore, having fastened on the belt of truth, and having put on the breastplate of righteousness…praying at all times in the Spirit, with all prayer and supplication. To that end, keep alert with all perseverance, making supplication for all the saints (Ephesians 6:13–14, 16–17).

The passage above urges us to be ready to "withstand in the evil day…to stand firm…praying at all times," and to "keep alert." All of this is made possible by "the whole armor of God"—that is, an armor that God Himself has provided. We are not left to fend for ourselves against the corrupt and wicked culture of our day. God has supplied us with what we need. That's why it's so crucial that we stay close to Him and place our complete reliance upon Him in all things.

A Hero Who Found No Reason to Hide

The apostle Paul warned about people who would pursue desire-driven theology, "having itching ears" that "accumulate for themselves teachers to suit their own passions, and will turn away from listening to the truth" (2 Timothy 4:3–4).

This has increasingly been the trend in today's churches. There are those who, with a misguided understanding of love and compassion, have sought to make the church more like culture rather than like Christ.

Read Romans 12:1–2: "Present your bodies as a living sacrifice, holy and acceptable to God… Do not be conformed to this world, but be transformed by the renewal of your mind." What are some ways Christians can easily and inadvertently find themselves conforming to this world?

What are some safeguards we can apply to keep that from happening?

Action Step

Think of specific unbelievers or discouraged believers you know. How would you rate your level of availability to them? What are some ways you can improve your availability, and what steps you can take to be a positive and gospel-focused influence on these people?

CHAPTER 8

Will We Oppose the Fiction of a Gender-Neutral Society?

One of Satan's most effective strategies for attacking people is to undermine the traditional family structure as designed by God.

Think about it: The marriage of a man to a woman and the birth of children to create a family are the two most foundational elements of human society. When God brought forth humanity, He started with the marriage relationship, then family relationships. From there, He expanded out to communities and to governments. The stronger that marriages and families are, the stronger communities and governments will be.

Conversely, when marriages and families fall apart or break from God's original design, then society falls apart too. Simply by tearing apart a marriage or a family, Satan can do widespread damage to communities and more.

At the core of the marriage and family units—as God designed them—are certain standards for gender and sexuality. When these are altered or undermined, havoc is unleashed. That is why the moral revolution has been so incredibly damaging. Culture's rampant confusion regarding gender and sexuality has been devastating. It's no accident that Satan strikes hardest in the areas of gender and sexuality, for as he does so, he is able to turn that which God created to be good into things that are corrupt and evil.

Ultimately, as Romans 1:24–25 says, Satan has worked overtime to get people to exchange "the truth about God for a lie" and to worship "the creature rather than the Creator." People have put themselves in God's place and decided to be pleasers of self rather than of God.

SEXUAL CONFUSION AND POLITICAL POWER

People are willing to persuade themselves to believe lies and
put common sense on hold in order to avoid being shamed.

No Reason to Hide, page 196

What is the goal of the confusion regarding gender and sex?

What unchanging truth is proclaimed in Genesis 1:27?

Can feelings or external physical alterations made to the body override what a person's internal chromosomal makeup says about their identity?

THE BLESSINGS OF DISCRIMINATION

Leftists claim they do not discriminate, but in reality, they do. How do we know this?

What are some ways that we as Christians should be careful and discriminating (from a biblical standpoint)?

THE CRUX OF THE MATTER

We must speak, but we must speak with care.

No Reason to Hide, page 202

On page 203 of *No Reason to Hide*, we read, *"It is better to be accused of being harsh than it is to tell lies with hushed tones of compassion, love, care, and thoughtfulness."* Why is this the case?

Give an example of this kind of love in action—what is a problem or viewpoint that needs correcting, and how can it be corrected truthfully with care?

SHOULD WE CALL PEOPLE BY THEIR PREFERRED PRONOUNS?

What three principles does Andrew T. Walker offer for navigating pronouns and names?

1.

2.

3.

What advice is given for employees with regard to diversity compliance?

We must allow for freedom of conscience among us,
but we must also ask this question: Are we willing to pay the
price of faithfulness to God and follow our conscience?

No Reason to Hide, page 205

POINTING TOWARD HOPE

What did Jesus say that suggests celibacy is not to be condemned?

What promise did God make to those who choose to remain single and live in holiness?

THE GOSPEL FOR A BROKEN WORLD

How should we as Christians respond to those who tell us they might be transgender or homosexual?

We must distinguish between accepting a person and approving of their conduct. Every human being is created in the image of God and deserves to be treated with dignity and respect, but not every human being deserves approval for their conduct and lifestyle. We can be welcoming even when we cannot be affirming.

Let us be gentle, respectful, and courteous. And truthful.

No Reason to Hide, page 207

What helpful words does James Emery White offer to those who truly have gender dysphoria?

What one or two points in this chapter of *No Reason to Hide* did you find most helpful for providing clarity with regard to gender issues?

A Promise to Carry with Us

> My brothers, if anyone among you wanders from the truth and someone brings him back, let him know that whoever brings back a sinner from his wandering will save his soul from death and will cover a multitude of sins (James 5:19).

What other wisdom does Scripture offer with regard to helping those who are struggling?

Galatians 6:1—

1 Thessalonians 5:14—

A Hero Who Found No Reason to Hide

Walt Heyer's account calls attention to the fact that those who struggle with gender issues—as well as other problems—may very well be dealing with traumatic hurts from the past that haven't been addressed. This alerts us to the need for sensitivity and to be a careful listener. According to the following passages, what comforting truths can we offer to such people?

2 Corinthians 12:9—

Hebrews 4:15–16—

Action Step

When it comes to matters relating to gender and sexuality, you may feel as though you have nothing to offer because you're not an expert or a counselor. But don't let that discourage you from reaching out. You may very well be the one person who, at a crucial moment in time, has something to say or can help in some constructive way. As a Christian, what are some things you *can* offer to someone who is looking for help?

CHAPTER 9

Will Our Children Be Indoctrinated by the Enemy?

To understand why the radical left is so anti-family and desires to exploit our children, we need to realize their thinking is based on Karl Marx's views about the family and children. You'll recall that Marx viewed people as being in one of two categories—oppressors or victims. He saw the traditional family structure—with the father as the head of the household—as oppressive upon mothers and children. And he advocated that children belonged to the state, not to their parents. Therefore, the state must do whatever it can to separate children from their parents at as early an age as possible.

At the time of this writing, school boards have been telling parents that teachers and schools are better informed about raising children than parents are. These same school boards have gone so far as to adamantly prohibit parents from knowing what is taught in the classroom, hiding the fact that Critical Race Theory and other objectionable worldviews are included in the curriculum.

This explains the growing trend toward laws that allow minors to have abortions and other medical procedures without their parents' consent. Schools promote views about sexual and gender issues in ways that encourage children to become sexually active at much too young an age. In multiple ways, parental authority is being bypassed, leaving parents in the dark as to what is happening with their children.

In these ways and more, the biblical design for family is being undermined and destroyed.

Children are becoming wards of the state, and parents are prohibited from having any input. And it's all done for the purpose of indoctrinating children with the views espoused by the radical left—to ensure that these views can be passed along to the next generation.

TO WHOM DO CHILDREN BELONG?

What views did Hitler have about children?

Why did Hitler close down all alternative education options for parents?

From your own personal experience, how influential would you say teacher figures can be in a child's life?

In your opinion, what are some reasons that parents know better than teachers what their children should and shouldn't learn?

If the unnatural is to be seen as natural, if wrong is to be seen as right, if what is shameful is to be celebrated, children must be led into a state of confusion, an upending of all they assumed was right and good. They must be told they are to make up their own mind about these matters, but the curriculum is designed in such a way that it will produce the ideological conformity that is expected. Those who resist will be identified and often shamed. "Make up your own mind" really means "Break away from what you have been taught at home or at church and agree with us!"

No Reason to Hide, page 217

THE COLLAPSE OF MORALITY AND DECENCY IN OUR PUBLIC SCHOOLS

Why does the radical left want to deaden children's consciences?

While children are "told" to make up their own mind about cultural matters, what is today's curriculum actually designed to do?

When the radical left says, "Make up your own mind," what do they really mean?

Teaching Sexuality

On page 218 of *No Reason to Hide*, we read that in today's schools, "a child's *autonomy* must supersede a child's *anatomy*." What is meant by this?

What are some reasons transgenderism is increasing in schools?

What can happen if parents who teach Christian values to their children are seen as abusers?

The Race Controversy

What is the intent of theories like Critical Race Theory?

Essentially, Critical Race Theory teaches that the solution to anti-black racism is anti-white racism. In your mind, what are the better and more biblical ways to address racism?

ARE FAITH-BASED SCHOOLS EXEMPT?

Why are terms like *mom* and *dad* being discouraged by some?

What is the problem with the secular doctrine of inclusivity?

LET US LAMENT FOR OUR CHILDREN

What are some of the disturbing statistics regarding childhood mental illness?

What can we do as parents to ensure our children have healthy childhoods?

In your opinion, why is it helpful for us as Christian parents to view our children as not being owned by us, but by God?

We as Christians must affirm the worth of all children. All children are loved by God, who is able to give them a hope-filled identity.

No Reason to Hide, page 227

MY PLEA TO PARENTS

In today's culture, the ideal for children may be alternate means of education. But if there are no alternatives, what can a parent do?

In what ways have you seen public schools hostile to Christian values?

What are some ways that we as Christian parents or grandparents can help offset negative cultural influences in the areas of race and gender?

A Promise to Carry with Us

I will open my mouth in a parable; I will utter dark sayings from of old, things that we have heard and known, that our fathers have told us. We will not hide them from their children, but tell to the coming generation the glorious deeds of the LORD, and his might, and the wonders that he has done (Psalm 78:2–4).

What are some "glorious deeds" God has done in your life that you could share about with your children or grandchildren?

A Hero Who Found No Reason to Hide

In the hero story, we read, "Sometimes talented children squander their giftedness and opportunities through fruitless, self-serving decisions. Other times, the most unlikely prospects are mightily used of God. All we can do is earnestly pray and help steer our children in the right direction."

What have you seen other parents or grandparents do that you thought was a good idea for helping to steer children in the right direction?

Action Step

Parents and grandparents can truly benefit from supporting and praying for one another. Are you actively doing that now? If yes, how can you improve in this area? If no, what are some steps you can take to get started?

CHAPTER 10

Will We Submit to the Great Global Reset?

Many people are curious about the future. While there's a lot we don't know, the Bible does provide a preview of what we can expect to happen during Earth's final days before Christ's return. In the Old Testament book of Daniel, we are provided a panoramic sweep of future history, including the world's final kingdom. In Matthew 24–25, Jesus Himself revealed the signs that would precede His second coming. The book of Revelation is filled with information about the last days, and there are many other passages elsewhere in Scripture that contain prophecies about the future.

One of the major themes that appears repeatedly in Bible prophecy is the fact our world will one day be ruled by a global ruler. And not only will he be powerful, but he will also be ruthless. In 2 Thessalonians 2:3, he is called "the man of lawlessness...the son of destruction." He will go so far as to proclaim himself to be God (verse 4). He will oppose everything that is good, including Christ—which is why he will be called the *anti*christ. And he will demand that everyone in the world worship him.

While we do not know who this ruler will be and how he will come into power, Bible prophecy gives us enough details to know we're headed toward a world where everything will be controlled on a global scale. What do we see happening around us today that serve as indicators we are on the path to a one-world empire?

THE PUSH TOWARD GLOBALIZATION

What is the worldwide COVID-19 pandemic being used as a pretext for?

What did a panel recommend to the World Health Organization?

What did Klaus Schwab, founder of the World Economic Forum, say about things getting back to normal?

What are globalists saying needs to be done to bring equity to the world?

According to [globalist] thinking, national sovereignty must give way to global sovereignty. America must relinquish its position in the world to create a stronger United Nations that has the economic, environmental, and political power to readjust living standards around the globe.

No Reason to Hide, page 237

A BORDERLESS WORLD

At the US border with Mexico, what is happening under the guise of compassion?

Why do you think today's woke culture is so eager to end the due process of citizenship?

WHAT DOES THE BIBLE SAY ABOUT BORDERS AND CITIZENSHIP?

What evidence do we see in Scripture that God taught the Israelites to distinguish between foreigners who posed a threat to their culture and those who didn't?

When the apostle Paul wrote about his Roman citizenship in Acts 21:39, what rights did he confirm he had?

What is the symbol of the church, and what is the church's message?

What is the symbol of government, and what is government's responsibility and message?

THE DEATH OF MONEY AS WE KNOW IT

What action has the Federal Reserve taken in an attempt to bring relief from COVID-19?

Why would globalists find a worldwide economic meltdown appealing?

What would be among the consequences of having a fully digitized currency?

HEIGHTENED CONTACT
TRACING AND SURVEILLANCE

What are among the effects predicted of an all-digital currency and vaccine mandates?

In light of the dangers of COVID-19, what might people have to be willing to surrender?

What kind of utopia is being promised to those willing to surrender their liberties?

What are the promises of this new "utopia"? Its proponents say it is the path to peace and prosperity for all people and the planet. It will put an end to poverty and lack of education; it will reduce inequalities and save the oceans and forests. In exchange for these "benefits," we will surrender our liberty, ingenuity, and personal decisions about our finances and values. Our chains will give us a sense of security.

No Reason to Hide, page 246

What is China's social credit system all about?

In your opinion, how do you see these globalist trends paving the way for the antichrist's one-world government?

LIFE WITHOUT FREEDOM

What is meant by the fact that up till now, the American government and its institutions have always practiced "informed consent"?

What are some ways you can see life changing when governments impose even more intrusive mandates in the days to come?

SUPERMAN: THE WORLD'S GREAT HOPE

What observation did Vladimir Putin make about artificial intelligence?

While the idea of being able to connect the brain directly to the internet seems to promise benefits, what are two or three serious drawbacks you believe could result from such a development?

THE FINAL REVELATION OF
THE EVIL HEART OF THE HUMAN RACE

According to Genesis 6:5, what happens when mankind is left unrestrained?

What observation did Jesus make about the end times in Matthew 24:37–39?

A Promise to Carry with Us

Great and amazing are your deeds, O Lord God the Almighty! Just and true are your ways, O King of the nations!...All nations will come and worship you, for your righteous acts have been revealed (Revelation 15:3–4).

What wonderful assurances do we have about the future in the following Scripture passages?

Matthew 16:27—

Colossians 3:4—

Revelation 11:15—

Three Heroes Who Found No Reason to Hide

When Shadrach, Meshach, and Abednego refused to bow to the image created by Nebuchadnezzar, they not only expressed confidence that God could deliver them, but they also said that even if God chose *not* to deliver them, they still wouldn't bow. They recognized that, from an earthly perspective, God doesn't always deliver His people. Though God is not obligated to inform us of why He acts in the ways He does, what are some possible reasons you can think of for God choosing not to deliver His people?

Action Step

In today's culture, many Christians are feeling pressured to conform. They are being compelled to surrender or sink rather than swim. What are some specific ways we can pray for our brothers and sisters in Christ who are being urged to compromise?

CHAPTER 11

Will We Accept the Blessing
of Gospel-Centered Suffering?

For those of us who live in countries that have faced little true suffering for Christ, the idea of facing persecution like that experienced by those in fiercely anti-Christian nations is difficult to imagine. In fact, the prospect of enduring such suffering can leave us feeling fearful.

Yet this is a reality that many Christians have faced through the ages and continue to face today in some parts of the world. Remarkably, these believers have considered their persecution to be a badge of honor, taking the attitude of the apostle Peter, who wrote, "Rejoice insofar as you share Christ's sufferings" (1 Peter 4:13). Just as Christ suffered for doing what was right, so will we. Jesus Himself said, "A servant is not greater than his master. If they persecuted me, they will also persecute you" (John 15:20).

It is hard to imagine suffering as a privilege and a blessing, but that is what we read in Matthew 5:11–12—again, from Jesus: "Blessed are you when others revile and persecute you and utter all kinds of evil against you falsely on my account. Rejoice and be glad, for your reward is great in heaven, for so they persecuted the prophets who were before you."

To be persecuted for Christ's sake puts us in good company—the prophets, the apostles, and countless saints through the centuries have suffered greatly or died for their faith. If you live in a country that knows some level of religious freedoms, you might never face much persecution, but for you to be aware of what is happening to your brothers and sisters in

Christ in other places—and to be praying on their behalf—will help you to live with more of an eternal perspective.

We can be canceled but the gospel cannot. Nothing can thwart God's will from being done; He will keep saving and calling out a people for His name's sake.

No Reason to Hide, page 263

As Christians, when we're pushed into a corner, how should we view our refusal to submit?

Rod Dreher wrote that "relatively few contemporary Christians are prepared to suffer for the faith, because the therapeutic society that has formed them denies the purpose of suffering in the first place, and the idea of bearing pain for the sake of the truth seems ridiculous."[5] What are two or three ways you think today's Christians have "insulated" themselves from recognizing that suffering for doing what is right is part of being a believer?

TOWARD A BIBLICAL
THEOLOGY OF SUFFERING

On page 266 of *No Reason to Hide*, we read, "I've been forced to realize that my view of suffering has been shaped more by my American experience than the Scriptures." What has your personal experience been, and where do you see room for growth in your understanding of suffering?

We Are Called to Suffer

What truth does Paul declare in Philippians 1:29–30?

What example did Christ leave for us, according to 1 Peter 2:21?

What are some reasons we might think we should be exempt from suffering?

Why do we prefer to think that, as Christians, we ought to be exempt from suffering? There are other Scripture passages that teach the truth that suffering for Christ is to be expected. In fact, one verse I have often pondered is, "All who desire to live a godly life in Christ Jesus will be persecuted" (2 Timothy 3:12). Might one reason for our relatively infrequent suffering in the Western church be because we have lived so much like the world that we face no real resistance from it?

To suffer for Christ is our calling, our privilege.

No Reason to Hide, page 267

What reminder does 2 Timothy 3:12 give us?

Sometimes Suffering for Christ Begins with Our Own Families

In Matthew 10:34–38, Jesus made the point that even families will be divided because of faithfulness to the gospel. How have you personally experienced this, or seen this happen in someone else's family?

On page 269 of *No Reason to Hide*, we read, "If there is division, let it always be about Him and not about us."

What would be examples of divisions that are about Christ?

What would be examples of divisions that are about us?

Suffering Strategically Positions Us for Special Blessing

What does it mean to look beyond what persecution does in the visible realm and see what it does in the invisible realm?

According to 1 Peter 5:10–11, how can we benefit from suffering?

What benefits came from Paul's thorn in the flesh (see 2 Corinthians 12:9)?

Suffering Gives Us the Opportunity to Show the Supreme Worth of Christ

In Hebrews 10:32–35, what response are we encouraged to have toward suffering?

What opportunity did Jesus see coming from His suffering and crucifixion?

How can we, as believers, show that Christ means more to us than life itself?

Even When We Are Thrown into the Hands of the Devil, We Are Still in the Hands of God

In what ways have you seen evidence of God's sovereignty in the midst of your own suffering?

What is significant about the fact Jesus told the believers at Smyrna that they would be in the hands of Satan for "ten days" (Revelation 2:9–10)?

There comes a time when wicked hands can do only so much,
and all the while, we are in the hands of our heavenly Father.
He holds us tightly even as the fire rages.

No Reason to Hide, page 274

All Suffering Will Be Adjudicated by the Supreme Court of the Universe

What are you able to determine about God's justice when you read Revelation 20:12?

What principle are we given in Romans 12:19?

How did Jesus respond to injustice, according to 1 Peter 2:23?

Suffering Is Not a Sign of Lack of Faithfulness, but Rather, the Proof of It

In Hebrews 11, we read about some heroes of the faith. What changes when we reach verse 35?

What is a willingness to suffer without a miracle—or deliverance—proof of?

We Must Fear God More Than the Flames

Though it's very unlikely we'll ever be burned at the stake, what are some costly ways we may find it necessary to prove our faithfulness to Christ?

A Promise to Carry with Us

No matter what happens in the course of our suffering, what can we take heart in, according to John 16:33?

Heroes Who Found No Reason to Hide

Read the account of Daniel Wong's family and the persecution they faced in China. In what ways are you inspired by their example?

Action Step

What are you doing right now to bring encouragement or help to those who are experiencing opposition to their witness?

What one or two ways could you commit yourself to growing in this area?

Jesus Teaches Us How to Run Successfully All the Way to the Finish Line

Our challenges are big, but they are not as big as our God.

No Reason to Hide, page 283

What encourages you most as you read Paul's words in 2 Corinthians 4:16–18?

On page 284 of *No Reason to Hide*, we read that "the invisible world is just as real as the visible, and even today, it must become the source of our motivation and joy." What realities about the invisible world—the things of God and the spiritual realm—help to motivate you and give you joy?

When faced with the cross, where did Jesus find His joy?

How would the following three principles apply to the circumstances you are presently facing in life?

"Don't look around"—

"Look only at Me"—

"Keep climbing"—

Remember, all that matters is what matters for eternity.

No Reason to Hide, page 287

Final Promises to Take with Us

Given your life circumstances right now, how can you apply 1 Timothy 6:12 and "fight the good fight of the faith"?

What comforts you most about the promise given in 2 Timothy 4:18?

Living as Citizens of Heaven While We Are Citizens of Earth[6]

M ost of the New Testament epistles were written to help believers know how to live in a hostile culture. Among the many words the apostle Paul wrote, he reminded us that "our citizenship is in heaven" (Philippians 3:20), which brings us to this question: How are we who are citizens of the city of God to live in the city of man?

The Greek word Paul used in Philippians 3:20 is *politeuma*, from which we get our word *politics*. He says that our citizenship, our politics, if you please, "is in heaven." For Paul to point this out helps us to recognize that we are dual citizens—that is, citizens of two different cities that have different values, different loves, and different lifestyles.

THE DIFFERENCES BETWEEN CITIZENS OF EARTH AND CITIZENS OF HEAVEN

Notice the contrasts between the two citizens:

1. We Walk in Different Directions

"For many walk, of whom I have often told you and now tell you even with tears, walk as enemies of the cross of Christ" (Philippians 3:18). We walk where our affection takes us, and the cross is despised by those who are of the city of man. To them, the cross is foolishness.

Perhaps Paul is not referring solely to ungodly pagans, but also to the Judaizers who claimed to embrace the cross but added to its message. They too were enemies of the cross, and their behavior made Paul weep. You do not have to be a pagan to be an enemy of the cross; you simply have to add human merit as a requirement for salvation. That also renders the power of the cross of no effect.

There are more enemies of the cross than those who say they are; some "friends" of the cross deny its message. They belong to the city of man, even though they profess to belong to the city of God.

2. We Have Different Desires

"Their end is destruction, their god is their belly, and they glory in their shame" (Philippians 3:19). Again, in context, Paul might be referring to the Judaizers who believed that what they ate (or did not eat) reflected the status of their relationship with God. The phrase "their shame" might refer to the rite of circumcision, which was said to be the mark of a true Jew. The Judaizers gloried in this ritual, thinking it put them on better terms with God when, in actuality, it didn't.

Again, this passage has a wider application. For many people, their god is their appetite; they choose to fulfill every craving of the flesh, whether it be eating, alcoholism, drugs, sensuality of every kind. They glory in that which should give them shame.

The citizens of the city of man are characterized by the pleasurable values of this world. They are deceived into believing that the things of Earth can keep their promises, or at least that they are the only things that really matter. One way or another, they do all they can to eke out some happiness as they walk life's road.

In contrast, citizens of the city of God have meat to eat of which others know nothing. They know that one does not live by bread alone, but by every word that proceeds out of the mouth of God. They are learning to be content with God. And they agree with the Puritans, who, in essence, said, "He who has God and everything else does not have more than He who has God alone."

3. We Speak Different Languages

When describing the inhabitants of the city of man, Paul wrote that their "minds [were] set on earthly things" (Philippians 3:19). Listen to what people say when they talk—the topics of their conversations seldom arise above the things of this earth.

As Jesus observed in Matthew 12:34, "How can you speak good, when you are evil? For out of the abundance of the heart the mouth speaks." A sinful heart cannot rise above itself; it will generate only sinful thoughts and words.

In contrast, the citizens of the city of God speak a different language. As pilgrims, our speech betrays us. We speak with the recognizable accent of heaven. We are disappointed when our earthly treasures are stolen, but we are not dismayed. We know the difference between the temporary and the permanent, between the seen and the unseen. We rejoice in that which cannot be taken from us.

4. We Have Different Aspirations

The citizens of Earth pin all their hopes on the things that come to them from Earth. They long for the assurance of more wealth, power, and personal aggrandizement. They believe that "you only go around once"—therefore, you must get all you can while you can. They are preoccupied with their possessions, their activities, their fashions, and other things of the world.

Citizens of heaven, however, look for the heavenly King. They eagerly "await a Savior, the Lord Jesus Christ, who will transform our lowly body to be like his glorious body" (Philippians 3:20). They look for Him because they love Him and are eager to "see him as he is" (1 John 3:2).

5. We Will Arrive At Different Destinations

Of those who belong to the city of man, Paul said, "[Their] end is destruction" (Philippians 3:19). They have chosen to alienate themselves from God in this life, and will be so in the life to come. In contrast, we who are citizens of the city of God await the return of Christ and the transformation of "our lowly body to be like his glorious body, by the power that enables him even to subject all things to himself" (verse 21).

Those who belong to the city of man are destined to separation from God and eternal condemnation. And those who belong to the city of God will live in God's presence and enjoy eternal life.

THE CHOICES WE HAVE AS
CITIZENS OF HEAVEN WHILE ON EARTH

For now, we who are citizens of heaven are still citizens of Earth—we are dual citizens. We are surrounded by a culture that is thoroughly at odds with God and His ways. So how are we to fulfill our obligations as dual citizens? We have three options.

First, we can withdraw. That was what the Mennonites and Anabaptists did during the Reformation era. They would have nothing to do with law enforcement, war, or politics. They preserved themselves by having as little contact with the world as possible. The arts, culture, and society in general were evil and to be avoided. They studied the Bible with those who agreed with them, and for the most part, abandoned the world to the devil.

Some Christians today advocate a withdrawal from politics, saying that no Christian can serve in the city of man without compromise and eventual absorption within the secular culture.

I disagree.

Second, there are those who tell us that we should capture the city of man through political power. We should overtake its institutions, its power base, and its courts. Then the city of God can rule over the city of man.

Today, some leaders tell us that we should "take dominion" of the earth by capturing its power structures and enforcing God's laws. They believe that political power can rescue us from the moral and spiritual oblivion to which we are moving toward. But is it really our responsibility to capture the city of man, overtake it, and make it into the city of God? Can we expect the citizens of the city of man to abide by the laws of the citizens of the city of God? Ephesians 2 describes unbelievers as "dead in…trespasses and sins," and they are "by nature children of wrath" (verses 1, 3). To impose God's standards on the ungodly does not bring real change.

The third view is that we must learn to serve both the city of man and the city of God, with the priority being our devotion to Christ. We must learn to be salt and light with such spiritual power that society will be changed from the inside out. This approach asserts that we be involved at all levels of society, but with a distinctly biblical agenda. This is done with the recognition that the gospel is the first mission of the church—this is the way of the cross. It is the way of humility, the way of repentance, and when necessary, the way of suffering.

We all grieve because our society is full of darkness and evil. And we are frustrated at the way culture has declared war on Christian values. But what else can we expect from the city of man? Why should we think that the cross would be attractive to the world when the Bible pointedly says that it contains a message that will be greeted with hostility? Remember Christ's words: "If the world hates you, know that it has hated me before it hated you" (John 15:18).

So what are we to do? We must remain steadfast and proclaim the truths that those in the city of man need to hear. We must declare the message that says only Christ can bring about change, restoration, and hope. Yes, we must fight, but we must do so in the manner that Christ did: He never wavered from His message of spiritual redemption in the midst of political and social abuses. Note that Christ came to Earth not to take over governments, but "to seek and to save the lost" (Luke 19:10).

Through the gospel, we can bring change that nothing else can. This is the message that is needed most in this confused generation. The citizens of heaven must remain faithful to doing what only the citizens of heaven can do. We must keep pointing beyond this life to the next and encourage others to join us on our pilgrimage to the eternal city of God.

Notes

1. As cited in Leonid Bershidsky, "Tech Censorship Is the Real Gift to Putin," *Bloomberg*, January 11, 2021, https://www.bloombergquint .com/gadfly/tech-censorship-is-the-real-gift-to-putin.

2. Rod Dreher, *Live Not by Lies* (New York: Sentinel, 2020), 17.

3. Dreher, *Live Not by Lies*, 15.

4. Michael P. Farris, *We Are Americans* (Scottsdale, AZ: Alliance Defending Freedom, 2021), 5.

5. Dreher, *Live Not by Lies*, 13.

6. The material in this appendix is excerpted and adapted from Erwin W. Lutzer, *Why the Cross Can Do What Politics Can't* (Eugene, OR: Harvest House, 1999), 21–31.

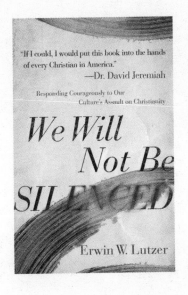

WE WILL NOT BE SILENCED

We Will Not Be Silenced prepares you to live out your convictions against a growing tide of hostility. Gain a better understanding of nonbelievers' legitimate hurts and concerns regarding issues like racism, sexism, and poverty—and identify the toxic responses secular culture disguises as solutions. In the process, you'll see how you can show compassion and gentleness to those outside of the faith without affirming their beliefs.

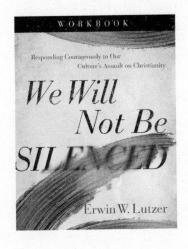

WE WILL NOT BE SILENCED WORKBOOK

This companion workbook to *We Will Not Be Silenced* gives you practical tools for responding to culture's hostility with Christlike strength and compassion, learning how you can best speak the truth with love. You'll be equipped to continue standing boldly for your faith and enriched in your understanding of how to do so effectively.

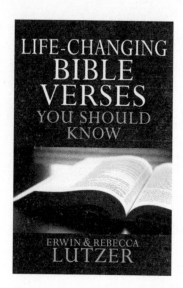

LIFE-CHANGING BIBLE VERSES YOU SHOULD KNOW
With Rebecca Lutzer

Do you desire to experience the life-changing power of God's Word? Do you long to hide God's Word in your heart, but don't know where to start?

In this book, Bible teacher Erwin Lutzer and his wife, Rebecca, have carefully selected more than 100 Bible verses that speak directly to the most important issues of life, and explained the very practical ways those verses can encourage and strengthen you.

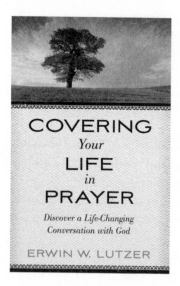

COVERING YOUR LIFE IN PRAYER

Every Christian longs for a better and more intimate prayer life. And one of the most effective ways you can grow more powerful in prayer is to learn from the prayers of others. In this book you'll discover new ways to pray—new requests, concerns, and thanksgivings you can bring to God's throne of grace. A wonderful resource for expanding your prayer horizons and enriching your relationship with God.

THE POWER OF A CLEAR CONSCIENCE

Do you struggle with feelings of guilt about your past? Or are you bogged down by a conscience that haunts or imprisons you?

This is not how God intends for you to live. Your conscience was not created to hold you prisoner, but to guide you and point you to freedom from guilt and bad habits. Longtime pastor Erwin Lutzer shares what it means to live in the power of a clear conscience as you

- learn how to deal with guilt and replace it with joy
- discover how the truth that can hurt you can also heal you
- realize the incredible extent of God's forgiveness and love for you

You'll find yourself encouraged by the truths that no failure is permanent and no life is beyond God's power to bring about change.

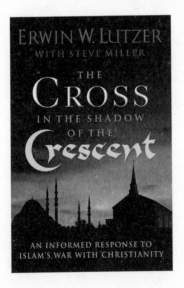

THE CROSS IN THE SHADOW OF THE CRESCENT

Islam is on the rise all over the West, including in America. In this compelling book, Erwin Lutzer urges Christians to see this as both an opportunity to share the gospel and a reason for concern. Along the way, you'll find helpful answers to these questions and more:

- How does Islam's growing influence affect me personally?
- In what ways are our freedoms of speech and religion in danger?
- How can I extend Christ's love to Muslims around me?

A sensitive, responsible, and highly informative must-read!